The END is Near,

Save U.S.

Christopher Zullo

ISBN: 153331053X

ISBN-13: 978-1533310538

INTRODUCTION

There is a quiet underlying but pivotal battle for the soul of our nation. Do money and ignorance rule, or will science and tolerance prevail? There has always been a quest for the human species, like ants, to explore new worlds and concepts. This growth does not just exist where we expand but in who we are and the knowledge we've acquired along the way. There have always been counter winds to that growth, whether it be greed, self-interest or our very nature; because one thing is always certain, our means of survival leads to our morality.

In recent years, with the rapid advancement of technology, I have seen these counter winds grow and become such powerful forces. Societal progress is no longer measured in our growth of knowledge, integrity, and character but in the acquisition of material goods. No longer taking pride in who we are and what we accomplish but instead relying on what we have and how complacent we are. How has this happened? Why does it matter? How can government help correct this problem?

"We no longer live in neighborhoods. We live in communities, not bound together by care for our neighbors but by self-interest and greed" - Christopher Zullo

Christopher Zullo

CONTENTS

Chapter 1: My beliefs

My name is Christopher Zullo. My story is a simple one. My Father was a teacher and professor, who became disillusioned with the educational system and the strict teaching methods that were not suited for individual students learning styles and needs. My mother was a political activist, fighting for women's rights; a feminist in her time. Culture and politics was and is still their glue. My parents grew up in a time when learning triumphed over wealth. The smartest man in the room, not the wealthiest was the most revered and respected. The most enduring quality I learned from my parents was the determination to learn: to figure shit out. You need to look at every angle, position, and fact to formulate an opinion. You don't always have to be right but have to come to the right conclusion and be able to defend it for your integrity.

"Anti-intellectualism has been a constant thread, winding its way through our political and cultural life, nurtured by the false notion that democracy means that 'my ignorance is just as good as your knowledge.'" – Issac Asimov

"The illiterate of the 21st century will not be those who cannot read and write but those who cannot learn, unlearn, and relearn." – Alvin Toffler

I've, over the years, learned this basic attitude towards life from learning two concepts, empirical evidence and the scientific method. Empirical evidence is information observed or acquired over time that compounds on itself, the source of knowledge acquired. The scientific method is a group of techniques designed to filter out bias and self-interest in scientific knowledge. It's a pattern used to ask questions, form a hypothesis and test those predictions. By understanding these concepts its allowed me to remain objective in my actions. How I think, learn and act. If I can validate my opinion, then have the knowledge to defend it no matter the propaganda, ad hominem or red herring, I'm validated in my purpose. Applying this model to two concepts of humanity has been a journey. My faith and government.

My faith has been one of importance because of the difficulty to verify and test. There is no authority on the matter, no person or thing that truly has the answers, but I have defined a system to come to the same answer time after time. I'm what I like to call an agnostic theist. Not classically defined but personally identified. There are at least seven religions, each with their individual deities and Gods. How did this happen? How could this happen? The answer is simple, but to come to its conclusions, you must start from the beginning and what is most prevalent in society and work your way backward.

To do this, I start at the beginning. Where did the traditions from religion develop? Who was the earliest foundation of man to exist? Why did he exist and what do we know about him? To date, at the publication of this book, that would be Homo Naledi.

"Teach your children about Homo Naledi. The first early human ancestor to use fire in caves and bury their dead" - Christopher Zullo.

These two traits, using fire to light

a cave and burying your dead, are two of the most basic actions of the human species; using knowledge to adapt to your environment and tradition to solidify your faith.

Faith. When someone has a conversation with me about religion, I always start with the same preface. If you want to talk to me about religion, let's start with biblical history. Most often, I find the most contentious conversations centered around Christianity, Islam, and Judaism. First, to define each, you have to look at why and how each came about.

Before technology and science, we had no knowledge of how or why things happened. Lightning, food availability, herds, crops, etc. could all

7

be used as fear-mongering tactics to support or destroy a belief that suited your position. You could blame any tragedy, thus, pushing your agenda, without evidence to support your position. It's a timeless tactic that still rings true today when you don't want to explore data, science or facts. Most often, religious beliefs were founded in paganism, in which you had multiple gods—gods of war, love, sea, etc.— to whom you prayed and celebrated, hoping for action from that deity on the particular topic and or problem at hand.

"Today's major religions were violent transitions from polytheistic worship to monotheistic worship" -Christopher Zullo

Judaism was formed from the

earliest record of the three. The Merneptah Stele described early Jewish ancestors, who were slaves under the pharaohs' rule in Egypt. They did nothing but build pyramids as tombs for these Pharaohs. They fled that slavery and settled in a city called Cannan. Pottery artifacts in this area confirmed the growth in population and the settlers attributed their freedom to one God; thus, their teachings of Judaism were formed.

Christianity started with a man. This man, Jesus, became upset with the Jewish temples. To conduct commerce and trade in this period, you needed a form of currency. These coins, minted by Jewish Templars, carried interest on its creation. How could they have the desire to profit off of the people and their needs to conduct trade while promoting their religion? Later in life, he challenged the Roman Empire, pagans, that his kingdom of heaven could provide better for the poor than the Roman Empire ever could. The Roman Empire determined this questioned their authority, and for the penalty, he was crucified.

Meanwhile, in the Middle East, drought and water security was the primary concern of Bedouin tribes. Multiple conflicts sprung forth over wells and their rights. Muhammed was tired of seeing conflict over these wells and brought peace through war conquering the region. He said he was just a man and not divine. The Islamic religion's schism between Sunni and Shia occurred after his death over lineage and leadership.

Once I looked at all these religions and their biblical histories, not their propaganda, I came to the long, hard conclusion that any god or deity would want the same things and tolerance of all. Religion brought peace to chaos, but traditions change over time based on socialization, needs and environment.

Systems of laws designed to give people a collective moral obligation to advance society was each's goal. Like our forefathers, who were deists, they ensured the foundation of society. The constitution, created and ratified by our forefathers was an advancement for rule by due process, rather than kings and clergy.

Throughout the ages, this has transferred into systems and roles of governments. Governments and its leaders can be incredibly powerful tools of good, designed to adapt its laws to the people's needs. This powerful force, combined with my passion for helping the suffering, sparked my interest in politics.

A program called Close-Up fueled began my interest. A group of students traveled to Washington, D.C., and discussed pertinent political issues of our time in groups and sub-groups. I remember debating whether we should bomb Saddam Hussein before the Gulf War and whether other ways to out the authoritative dictator, like assassination, were plausible.

Model United Nations taught me about global politics and the balance between each nation and their sovereignty. Technology and intellectual property were the most intriguing. One country, holding an advancement, could be the salvation of another. I wanted to bridge the divide between humanity and greed, which compelled me to think about the bigger picture in global and domestic politics.

I was raised in the era of technological revolution. My father had an Apple IIc, with floppy drives, in the basement. My video game console of choice was the Sega Genesis.

Geopolitical war games were my favorite. My mother, in this technological revolution, formed a business, which would lay a foundation to my own. One day, I saw a list of orders that had been sent via. fax. The orders were all generated on the internet, thus, fueling my ambition. From there, I began my journey in website design, internet marketing and social media.

I was never good at taking tests; reciting information, over and over again, only to be tricked by multiple choice questions. I often had more questions than answers; so, in college, I focused on my business. Over the years, I've become a self-made man, directing millions in advertising and generating tens of millions in sales. More importantly, this experience, without a degree, has helped to teach me the balance between people, government and business.

The role of government vs. business is a delicate one. Throughout human history, this balance has changed over and over again. What should be the role of government in business? In its citizenry? Over half of human history was ruled by kings and tyrants that led their people. They controlled trade and private enterprise, levied taxes to pay for wars, and distributed land for loyalty. Democracy eventually took hold, and economic systems began to define themselves into three categories.

Capitalism and socialism are both market-based systems with socialism putting the people's necessities for survival in the government's control. Communism, which is a command economy, exercised centralized government control. Capitalism highlights private ownership of industry and individual economic freedom. Communism puts private property and industry in governments control. Socialism is a hybrid of the two putting means of production in the people's hands but control of wealth, and its distribution lies to the government.

My beliefs toward government and economic systems have taken foundation in several principles. Science is fact. There is nothing that disputes it. 1+1=2, and when you combine two hydrogen molecules with an oxygen molecule, you make water. Everything can be measured and tested. Political policy is an evolving set of legislation based on need. Being wrong and being able to admit fault is just as important as being right. Getting lucky in life is a combination of hard work meeting opportunity.

Because of these principles, I find myself believing in a quasi-system of capitalism, with regulation and controls enacted by the people's representatives. I find people behaving like ants building an ant hill. We all strive to reach the same goals or new heights but need each other along the way to accomplish our socialized reality of life and corresponding success. The drive created by capitalism and its freedom helps propel us and these desires. The space race with the Soviet Union was one such example. The Soviets used space as propaganda to its people on why communism was better than capitalism. In my view, capitalism made space a dream to man, engulfing our minds and hearts.

With capitalism, there lies a flaw. Absolute power corrupts absolutely, and greed can lead those to gouge society on the whole for self-interest and profit. Eventually, you become greedy, losing sight of where you came from or hurt others to maintain the very success you worked to achieve. Communism and socialism have the same flaws, but to the extreme plight of the people because of power placed in the governors, not the governed. Capitalism has controls that can be used to offset these flaws and serve as a social safety net. We've passed regulations like progressive taxation, unions, minimum wage, workfare, and social security. These laws prevent the hoarding of wealth by the privileged few and protect the people from corporate greed.

These beliefs, most often, define me as a Regulatory Capitalist and part of a long-deceased political group that is most aligned with modern Democrats: Rockefeller Republicans. Rockefeller Republicans, in the modern sense, are dead. Many try to classify "liberal republicans" into this group, but they do not espouse the true nature of progressive politics that we support. The government role is to protect the people and regulate corporations, not protect corporations and regulate people. Rockefeller Republicans opposed socialism and government ownership but supported regulation and New Deal social programs. Unions are important parts of the economy because they protect worker rights and wages while infrastructure provides the engine for growth. Unions provide organized bargaining power against corporate greed. Regarding diplomacy, you spoke softly and carried a big stick. Military action was the last, not the first resort.

My civic duty, throughout
the years, has adapted several forms.
As a teenager, I had watched, in
shock, as George Bush, Sr. tried to assert
direct military-political influence over
the middle east. I was shocked when Bill
Clinton, my idol, the explainer-in-chief
who worked with Congress to balance
the budget and usher in a
technological revolution, lost his self-
control to sexual desires. I was truly
disappointed when the Supreme Court
handed George W. Bush Jr. the office
of the presidency, which in turn
destroyed the intellectual nature of the
presidency. The power of propaganda
and greed is shaping our nation despite
attempts by President Obama to
rescue us with good policy and role

model leadership.

Chapter 2: the End is Near, Save U.S.

The writing is on the wall. I see it; you feel it: the end of American exceptionalism, society as we know it — quite possibly the human race. These things have been predicted many times in history, but this is it, the point at which our advancement in science and knowledge can make or break us as a species. Growth is no longer a logistical one but an internal struggle, its expansion limited by time and place.

There's no more final frontier for us to expand. Wild West. Great unknown explored. The stars no more excite us as a species us but make us feel small, limited. What's our meaning, purpose, reason to be?

Life is like economies of scale from atoms to ants to humans. Habitual and random actions with tilts toward survival and preservation of the status quo. The instincts of basic survival have been replaced by the need to be recognized and succeed; with social media pushing an internal materialistic vs. internal self-worth struggle. Success is no longer measured by your integrity and charity as you climb the path to success but by your peer's comparison, acceptance, and recognition.

You are placated by a selfish desire to acquire goods no matter the cost to who or what, whenever and wherever, ignoring collateral damage along the way. The most dangerous being those who become entitled and will do anything to maintain that status.

Let's look at what we've done and are doing to our home. No, not the where we sleep but to our environment, our planet. It's our only one, colonization of another a distant non-reality due to time and distance to get there. Traveling faster than the speed of light is not a realistic concept with our bodies' physical limitations.

Our planet and its life exist with the most basic of foundations, the carbon cycle. Carbon's role in life is the most significant of all elements. It exists in all biological compounds and minerals. This carbon cycle is the exchange of carbon between the atmosphere and life. This sequence of events is critical to the earth sustaining such carbon-based life. We, by definition, are carbon-based lifeforms.

Fossil fuels themselves are the biological sequestration of carbon, meaning that extra carbon is stored in their biological material. This process is a natural process and is responsible for the extensive coal and oil deposits that exist on our planet. When burned, this carbon and extra energy are released to create electrical power through motion. This cheap form of energy creation was discovered in the 1820's and has been abused since. The byproduct of this activity is the excess carbon which is released when burned. Where do you think it goes? Right into our atmosphere.

"We've damaged the environmental carbon cycle by releasing (burning) millions of tons of sequestered carbon (fossil fuels)." – Christopher Zullo

These fossil fuels in and of themselves are a limited resource, formed over time and their availability a constant argument. Even the most liberal estimates place world oil reserves at 100 years, and that includes the refinement of shale, which is fine-grained sedimentary rock from which oil can be extracted and is not truly oil. Extracting shale, in and of itself, is a desperation move for oil production. The environmental impact of shale takes more land, waste to be disposed of, increased water use, and increased carbon emissions.

"Can't base effective long-term energy policy off finite resource. We have 99 years of oil left, including shale." – Christopher Zullo

The increased carbon in our atmosphere affects our environment. When there is increased carbon in the atmosphere, it retains additional heat. This extra heat impacts weather patterns, ocean chemistry, and ice cores. In the last two decades, we've experienced the hottest fifteen of sixteen years in human history[1].

Weather patterns are becoming more extreme, storms stronger and less predictable. Ocean acidification is destroying sea life, including coral, and glaciers are melting at an alarming rate. Half of animal species have been wiped out since 1970[2], one in six face extinction[3], and global carbon dioxide levels measured in parts per million are at 397 when the maximum concentration deemed sustainable to sustain life over the long term is 350[4].

Climate deniers argue human impact on this process, but that itself is a false equivocation when looking at science. Emissions of carbon dioxide into the atmosphere exceed these natural fluctuations. Carbon dioxide levels in the atmosphere have exceeded measurements from the last 420,000 years[5].

With human population growth, the burning of millions of tons of sequestered carbon has placed a heavy burden on our planet. Drinking water is essential to human life and its impact on society is profound. Every human being needs 100 gallons of water a day to survive[6]. One pound of beef takes 1,779 gallons of water to produce[7]. Drought and chronic water shortages impact 1.2 billion people and water use is growing at more than twice the rate of population increase[8]. Forty percent of all rivers in the United States and 46 percent of all lakes have become so polluted that they're no longer fit for human use[9]. It's estimated that the state of California itself only has one year supply of fresh water left[10].

Look at the Middle East as an example, where because the lack of irrigation systems, you wipe with your right and shake with your left to prevent spreading disease. We've created huge corporate farming operations around the world and are consuming more than half of our available calories from meat, when it's suggested that only a small amount should be part of our daily caloric intake[11].

"Animal husbandry has major environmental impacts and heavy water consumption. Need waste management and food planning" – Christopher Zullo

Beyond the destruction of our environment because it's cheap, easy, and has made many rich, the greatest threat to our individual liberty has changed from not having the freedom to pursue our dreams to not having the means to accomplish those pursuits. The wealthy and successful have been put into a trance of never-ending acquisition of goods and consolidation of power, where their diluted vision of survival relates to their subsequent fear of losing status. We must remember that wealth is not just money in the bank, but the value placed on all goods and resources on this planet, including land.

This gross income inequality has created a vacuum of acquisition and manipulation to advance those interests. Self-interest and greed have become so prevalent and respected in society that it's no longer looked at like it should, as evil. We espouse it in our children and in our dreams, being diluted to think anyone can obtain it with just hard work. But like becoming a professional sports player, there is more in genetics and who your parents are than just hard work.

Most of those who obtain this elite status should struggle with their internal demons of guilt but most often cling to the survival-of-the-fittest excuse as their means of acceptance. The saddest part of this whole cycle is that selflessness is being taken over by selfishness like a drug that makes you feel good but destroys your body.

The top 1% own 75% of all US financial assets[12],400 Americans have more wealth than half of all Americans combined[13], and the richest 1% now has as much wealth as the rest of the world combined[14]. Eighty people hold the same amount of wealth as the world's 3.6 billion[14]. The wealthiest 400 Americans have a combined wealth of over $2 trillion dollars[15]. That $2 trillion could employ 13 million Americans for five years at $30,000 per year.

"Freedom means nothing without liberty and the greatest threat to liberty is income inequality." – Christopher Zullo

This self-interest and greed have begun to corrupt the major aspects of our journalistic and political process. Journalists are forced to report the most inflammatory speeches and events for networks to increase ratings and attract advertisers, and politicians are beholden to their donors for funds to run their re-election campaigns.

"Corruption of our journalistic and political process by self-interest and greed is the issue of our time." – Christopher Zullo

The average cost to win a seat in the House of Representatives lies at $1.7 million, and Senate seat at $10.5 million[16]. Super PAC influence has dwarfed that in comparison. In 2012 609,417,654 was spent by super PACs, $345,163,595 in 2014 and $438 million to date in 2016 with a 5-1 ratio on conservative vs. liberal ideologies[17].

These financial needs and powers have repercussions in the form of legislation designed to benefit their donors rather than the people they represent. Just look at some of the impacts that the wealthy and well-connected have been able to accomplish by slanting legislation. In 1976, the 1% earned 8.9% of all income[12]; in 2012, they earned 22.46%[12]. In 1950, corporations paid $3 in taxes for every dollar paid by a worker. Now they pay less than 50 cents[17]. Of the Fortune 500, 111 companies paid zero dollars in federal income tax in at least one year from 2008-2012[18]. The richest 1% paid an effective federal income tax rate of

22% in 2014 while someone making an average of $75,000 paid a 19% rate[19]. The average federal income tax rate of the richest 400 Americans is just 20% percent[19], and corporate profits alone are nearly twice our government's annual budget. These numbers only continue to get worse with every year, and as the wealthy horde more and more, our federal and consumer debt totals both rise near upwards of $35 trillion dollars[20] while corporations and the 1% evade taxes at home and abroad.

"Taxes are dues we pay for the privileges of membership in an organized society." – Christopher Zullo.

"Progressive taxation ensures greed and poverty do not beset opportunity

and freedom. When eroded you create generations of entitled wealthy and a disenfranchised middle class" – Christopher Zullo.

This gross inequality, beyond its corruption on our process, wealth, and debt, is having a wide-ranging impact on our daily lives. Jobs, inequality, employment, poverty, retirement, and education are the most affected.

"When you see a closed down business, it wasn't taxes or regulation that shut them down. It was lack of consumer demand" – Christopher Zullo

Technology itself has helped fuel this inequality. Manufacturing used to be a great staple of economic growth, but with the advent of robotics and the assembly line, we eliminated the need for employees at middle-class wages. For a one-time cost of $40,000 and only $1 hour to maintain, with 24-hour work shifts and no benefits, human labor is becoming expendable. Even at the point of sale, more and more businesses are turning to automated check-out lanes, replacing workers.

Labor participation decline levels are due to these technological innovations. This impact is trickling down into early retirements, adults going back to school to learn new skills, and an aging population. This is making education more necessary in order to earn a middle-class wage, making college not just an option, but a necessity.

Apprenticeship and trade craftsmanship are slowly dying with internships being increasingly used to avoid costs. Small business is no longer looked at in terms of the means of production but rather franchising off a larger corporate entity to provide a service. Job growth is occurring at the lower wage service sector as profits increasingly drive corporate decision-making. No longer is the decision made to hire based on demand but rather the maximum probability.

"You can't reduce dependence on government services when you protect corporation's ability to pay low wages" – Christopher Zullo

"With modern technological innovation, computers, robotics and

electronics; we're eliminating jobs.
Ignored, this problem will only get
worse" – Christopher Zullo

These issues have created some major inequalities with minorities for job opportunities and incomes, forcing a much larger segment of their populations to rely on lower paying jobs. When the percentage of Hispanic and African-American children living in poverty is beyond 20%[21], there is a systematic underlying problem. In the Fortune 500, only 4% of CEOs are minorities[22]. Only 14.6% of small business owners are African-American and only 10% Hispanic[23].

This is a true example of trickle-down suffering with lower wages and less job growth. Most often this forces families to rely on one another to survive, creating a system that inadequately provides a lack of opportunity, ultimately leading to crime, drug use, and violence.

"Racism itself is a byproduct of intolerant socialization of youth and long term poverty combined with lack of opportunity" – Christopher Zullo

"Poverty is not just a momentary situation but a perpetual cycle of despair and lack of opportunity" – Christopher Zullo

This poverty and inequality often boil over into our police force as communities are torn apart by drug use, gangs, and violence. This increase in crime strains our police force and puts pressure on the community to act. We need more police officers with better training, pay, benefits, and local accountability with local community hiring. This inequality is the foundation for the racial tensions we see bubbling over time and time again.

"When 1 in 4 black males will spend time in prison there is a systematic problem of representation and due process" – Christopher Zullo

Modern science is exploding the lifespan of human beings. In the 1900s for example, the average lifespan in the US was about 45 years for both men and women[23]. Now it has exploded to about 75 years[23]. As we live longer, our needs increase over time, and our productivity decreases. Social Security and Medicare were designed as part of a system to help alleviate the stress of an aging population. By the entire country investing in its future, we would be able to take care of our elders and, at the same time, remain a growing and productive economy.

Unfortunately, over the years there has been an assault on these services. Many want to privatize the system and increase the age of eligibility for benefits; which would put those who need social security and Medicare at risk of complete poverty and certain death. These services have often become the only means of survival for many seniors.

"The United States is home to 5% of the world's population but 25% of its prison

population" – Christopher Zullo

"We should be strengthening Social Security benefits not raising the retirement age or risking it in Wall Street" – Christopher Zullo

Meanwhile, the notion of a well-educated populace, which our founding fathers insisted was critical to our nation's survival, is slowly disappearing. Inequality can be seen in test scores based on zip codes while property tax funding is creating an unequally educated society.

The scores of African-American children are nearly 40 points lower than those of Caucasians in science and 30 points lower in math.

Fear-mongering has become the

norm rather than the fringe behavior it once was. Just looking at the most electric topics of abortion, immigration, terrorism, guns, and the constitution itself, you find extreme ideological beliefs driving certain individuals beyond rational thought, fueled by the media's incessant need to promote this for ratings and advertisers.

No one likes abortion, but it happens whether its legal or not. We've learned this throughout history. A woman's right to choose and not be emotionally attacked for this right is crucial. Men's control over women has been one of the most undiscussed struggles since civilized society started taking shape. Many fought and died for women's suffrage. Women are not men's property or theirs to control. Even today laws exist that you'd think were still written in barbaric times. Personhood amendments are forcing women to bear the offspring of rapists, and in more than ½ of American states, they have the right to sue for child custody[25]. Contraceptive use and education are how we prevents abortions, not clinging to ineffective abstinence programs. I don't like abortion; I personally believe that after 20 weeks, abortion should not be an option unless it's rape, incest, or a case of the mother's life. However, it has to remain safe, legal, and in a doctor's office.

"Before abortion was a legal medical procedure desperate women often

resorted to poison, abuse and blunt objects." – Christopher Zullo

"When women are raped and you to take away their right to an abortion it forces them to bear offspring of rapists." *– Christopher Zullo*

"By scientific definition spermicide and birth control are abortion. Life begins at conception, not for ideological gain." – Christopher Zullo

Weapons to protect yourself have been instrumental since the bronze age, but their uses and role in modern society has changed over the years. The Second Amendment was written in a time when we had no regular army to protect us from foreign invasion and governments had no checks and balances. Today, for some, weapons are not just looked at as a tool to prevent invasion but a necessary power for their psychological security against others and government.

In my belief, security should be largely tasked to the military and police force: The military to prevent foreign invasion and ensure national security, and the police force to enforce justice and prevent civil unrest. Our votes and democracy have become the tool to prevent government corruption. No amount of assault rifles will take down a tank or stop a drone strike. Background checks prevent those who shouldn't have weapons from acquisition. This is protecting our freedom, not hampering it. Checks should be universal except for law enforcement officers/military and by God, if we don't trust you to board an airplane, you should in no way own an assault rifle.

"I'd rather have more cops on the street with better training, pay, and benefits than an armed military populace" – *Christopher Zullo*

"If a child threw a rock at another child on a playground, should we arm every child on that playground with a rock? Would more kids throw rocks or less?" – *Christopher Zullo.*

This leads me to our Constitution. Our Founding Fathers wrote the Constitution as a living document, with their greatest attempts to build the ability for it to mold over time. Today, strict Constitutionalists often use the document as a punch line to hardline supporters so they may advance personal agendas. We must stop using our Constitution as a hammer against each other but as a roadmap with interpretable cases based on our current situational needs.

"Freedom of religion exists to protect your rights, not impose them on others. Your freedoms end where another's begin. You can't yell fire in a crowded theater with the expectation that your speech is protected" – Christopher Zullo

"Without liberty, due process, and the Bill of Rights, my freedom means nothing." – Christopher Zullo.

As we built this great nation on

opportunity and rights, we were the envy of the world. With this envy, you have those who wish to join our country. Even our Founding Fathers left their own nation in search of a better life, the same way many immigrants do today in a much harsher and more technological climate. Very few of us are Native Americans, and the ones who are have been isolated from society on reservations and had their traditions destroyed.

With technology erasing our borders both physically and culturally, we are becoming a global community. When this happens, customs and traditions begin to clash, and you have the stronger dominating the weak. Currently, there are near 14 million

Americans living in the shadows, working and raising their families among us. These 14 million don't have any of the documentation that comes along with being a citizen, drivers licenses, and social security cards, and thus, most often, they resort to illegal means to survive.

"Love for country from those not of its birthright is the measure of your nation's success." – Christopher Zullo

This immigration problem is not just a United States problem. Over the past century, as distances become less a barrier, we've become a global economy engaging in massive amounts of trade. With this, we've become co-dependent on each other's resources and labor to produce the products and services we need. With globalization, many conflicts of interests between different government styles and corporations have ensued. By our inherent nature, these conflicts help poverty and inequality spread, with one side always coming out ahead, thus breeding violence for control of what remains. This violence is often nationalist in nature but regresses to a form of religious zealousness, as those in poverty most often turn to their local traditions and religious leaders for guidance.

One of the largest schisms that have developed in the modern world is the conflict between Islam and capitalism; which is most often tied to Christianity in Middle Eastern and

Western purview. With wars largely no longer fought by tanks but propaganda and terror, we've entered a psychological battlefield. Terrorists most often target not the military industrial complex, as they know they have no means of competing, but the people and their internal security.

How did this conflict come about? We must first look to the Crusades. Christians gathered large religious-based armies to try and conquer Christ's Holy Land and maintain control. Islam's formation along Christianity created a holy war conflict mentality during the period, as traditions, which dictated how we lived more in the Middle Ages, were at conflict. After the Crusades, there was a fragile symbiotic relationship between the two, most often with mosques and cathedrals being close to their respective populations. When world war broke out, it became a global affair with nations scrambling for strategic territory and resources (oil), and countries siding with each other for self-interest. We armed those sympathetic to the allies in Arabia to fight the Germans with tanks, artillery, and weaponry they most often had never seen. Then, when the world wars ended and the Cold War began, we started to arm the most ardent of those to fight a proxy war on our behalf against the Soviet Union with guerilla tactics and even more advanced weaponry. This bled the Soviet Union financially and caused a revolution against communism.

What happened after this you ask? We left. We let them struggle amongst themselves for control. Totalitarian dictatorships became entrenched as their individual power and control transcended the religious schisms of Shia vs. Sunni violence. We started investing in the region for favors and access to cheap oil, with military funding to states like Israel and Saudi Arabia. Imagine if the British convinced the French to take a more active role against us during the Revolutionary War. When we decided to invade Iraq instead of focus on the hunting of Bin-Laden, you saw the powerful impact of oil and the splintering of local terrorist groups into ISIS, which used a tormented Syria for recruitment and battlefield. The anger from groups in the Middle East boiled over to Western capitalism as the source of poverty and plight, with religion being their propaganda, and the promise of a better life fueling their resolve for conflict.

The more we stoke the fires of intolerance, hate, and xenophobia, the more we cloud the driving force of terrorism, poverty. Religious traditions mold themselves over time to conform to society and its needs.

For example, looking at human right violations, you see more and more in the Middle East as it is an attempt to cling to those traditions and beliefs.

Christianity itself had the same struggles during the inquisition when nearly 30,000 were killed because of their blasphemy[26], and during the KKK's peak, nearly 20% of white Christian males were part of hanging 3,500 African American[27]s. Less than 2% of Muslims identify with an extremist group[28], and majority of terrorist attacks occur in the Middle East, while their fellow Muslims are the target. Blaming an entire religion for the actions of extremists is how you create more terrorists, not fight terrorism.

"What happens when you wage campaigns in the name of Christianity, arm Arabia to fight the Germans, Taliban, the Soviet Union, and then invade IRAQ as interventionists?" –

Christopher Zullo

"My dream for the Middle East is Saudi Arabia, Israel, Egypt, Turkey, and Iran agree in the fight against Islamic extremism." – Christopher Zullo

"You advance freedom and democracy around the world by putting a Starbucks on every street corner, not a shoulder-powered anti-aircraft missile." – Christopher Zullo

"A major source of terrorism is poverty and nation building by armament, pitting Islam and countries against each other" – Christopher Zullo

Chapter 3: Soul of our nation

From monarchies to democracy, history is cycles of governments and their control over people. The struggle of oligarchs, plutocrats, and aristocrats usually determines society's stability, strength, and longevity.

As I mentioned before, there's a saying that transcends government type or structure: Power corrupts, absolute power corrupts absolutely.

When you are given the power to make laws; that power, unchecked, will grow exponentially to maintain and expand control, eventually corrupting every part of the nation to be controlled by the wealthy and well connected, not by the will or needs of the people.

In my definition, modern-day oligarchs can be defined as a group that bends government towards their will and self-interests. So, for example, if 90% of the population supported everyone getting free tacos on Tuesday but the government refused to pass it, you could be considered under the rule of oligarchs, governing by the will of the powerful, not the people.

Similarly, modern-day plutocrats can be defined as the same, but I see them as a different breed.

They are separated from the governing process but control extreme wealth. Most often, in becoming that wealthy, you have assets or customer bases that are affected by government legislation. With that being the case, you wish to exert control on such legislation to your favor.

With the government moving in the opposite direction of structured public campaign financing, we've seen plutocrats and oligarchs come together to truly stall the political process. Filibuster as long as you can get votes and your special interests can fund your campaign. This direction has allowed the industries that do the most damage with the least regulation to fight for the most control of legislation direction by special interest groups who make the largest donations.

By themselves, oligarchs have been somewhat limited in their growth through modern democracies. The better written a constitution, the better it is power-balanced to protect the will of the people. Plutocrats have always tried to buy their way into the influence of legislation - subsidies, controls, tariffs, etc. The reduction of royal families and the focus on checks and balances has helped create solid, long-lasting governing bodies for the people.

Recently, the emergence of modern-day aristocrats is attacking the fabric of society. The billionaire class who are no longer just highly sought after by the political class for donations but now themselves decide to delve into the political process and public office. Two such examples are Michael Bloomberg and Donald Trump. These politicians who are so closely tied to assets, taxes, and regulation seek to ascend to power, which puts us on a very dangerous path of corrupted leadership for their self-interests.

Until recently, champions of campaign finance reform had been holding the line. John McCain himself used to fight to keep money's influence out of politics, though he doesn't speak much about that anymore. Citizens United allowed the uber wealthy to wage campaigns on behalf of their politicians – how wild.

"Thanks to outside spending filtered through unlimited donation, Super PAC's special interests have been able to exert over $2 billion dollars of control through our leaders" – Christopher Zullo

"We need a new philosophy in government, not just separation of church and state but separation of corporation and state" – Christopher Zullo

Beyond the political processes corruption, the journalistic process is under assault. News used to be boring. But then came along entertainment news. 60 minutes was a pioneer, where news became a business. Once networks determined news could be profitable, their programming started to become tailored for appeal to the demographics that advertisers wanted to spend money to reach. This slowly has manipulated the journalistic process to reporting breaking news that exists outside our social norms. The age-old saying of "light your hair on fire and everyone will watch" news mentality has taken over any sense of reporting.

You have three major news networks that cater to every advertiser's demographic base. MSNBC caters for the left, Fox News the right, and CNN tries to walk the tightrope of broad appeal although they are often lumped into the "liberal media narrative." The one network that has gone above and beyond for ratings is Fox News, becoming more of a reality TV show based news network revolving around fear-mongering by highlighting inflammatory speech. This reporting with the combination of social media has created an ignorant confidence in one's own opinions and beliefs solidified by group acceptance.

"The corruption of our political and journalistic process by the 1%'s self-interest and greed in the issue of our time" – Christopher Zullo

"Money has corrupted our political process. Not by evil intent but by systematic corruption of greed and self-interest" – Christopher Zullo

With the political and journalistic process under assault, you turn to your scholars to hold society together. Education, knowledge, science; facts that are supported, promoted,

and can withstand opinion

due to their having higher credibility.

That class in and of itself is under siege.

With the underfunding of

the education, arts, and science

infrastructure, the expansion of money's

power over the community continues

to grow. Funding is more often used to

manipulate the findings that support

who is paying for the research. Scholars

are drowned out, and the ignorance

towards science is spreading. The age

of debate is no longer embraced.

Objectivity is diminishing. Socialization is

moving towards inflammatory

speech and traditions rather than

tolerance and scientific expansion. Fear

mongering prevents your frontal lobe

from being able to deduce rationally, making you easier to control.

"What has happened to our scholars? The scientific method and empirical evidence are vital to mankind's survival" – Christopher Zullo.

"The key to our nation's future resides in a well-educated populace, not red herring, rhetoric-driven sound bites that by those trying to lead and deceive" – Christopher Zullo.

Chapter 4: Our history

"To know who you are, you have to know where you come from. To know where you're going, you have to know who you are." – Christopher Zullo

We started out like wild animals similar to Neanderthals. We hunted by brute force with simple stone tools, with no language art or higher-level thinking. Neanderthals began to disappear as modern humans, the homo- species, came to evolve. This evolution occurred as we moved around the planet attempting to adapt to our constantly changing environments. Struggling to survive, we banded together and began to hunt in teams, which led to the eating of raw meat and the creation of food security. The consumption of raw meat shrunk our digestive tracks, which allowed our brains to grow, thus allowing traditions and routines to evolve.

Fire was one of the first technological advances, which allowed human expansion and environmental control. We could light the darkness, cook our food, scare away predators and much more. Fire was discovered in the plains of the Savanah, where lightning strikes sparked fires in the plains, which ancient humans eventually harnessed and learned to replicate.

With these advances, we began to record knowledge on cave walls. With these writings, we gained the ability to pass knowledge from one person to another, recording our history and advancements. With this, our desire to expand began to take hold. We explored different temperate zones and spread around the globe. With this expansion, ancient humans began to undergo physical changes to evolve, like shedding hair.

A major technological advancement that fueled human expansion and growth was the creation of papyrus in Egypt. With this, we began to develop a system of writing and the ability to communicate over distances. Different systems of languages and writings evolved over time and spread across the globe. In this period, a group of slaves escaped from the pharaoh's rule to establish ancient Israel.

The Phoenicians created the alphabet, which brought together languages and allowed the advancement of Ancient Greeks into mathematics. During this rapid period of technological advancement, many notions of the world were discovered through scientific discovery.

The greatest civilization in History, the Roman Empire conquered two-thirds of the modern world. They accomplished this through the development of roads, which allowed quick movement between cities. Military advances in troop training and tactics helped ensure their superiority.

During this period, Jesus challenged the Roman Empire and their Pagan Gods, that his Kingdom of Heaven could provide better for the poor than the Roman Empire. This was considered an act punishable by death and led to his crucifixion and the explosion of Christianity.

When the Roman Empire fell from corruption, the great libraries of Alexandria were burned, and knowledge was damaged. Thankfully, Arabian and Jewish scholars had made copies which allowed the transfer and preservation of knowledge.

Arabians came from a desert existence where water was their most treasured resource and the killing of each other over water rights was commonplace. Muhammed united the tribes of the desert through war. After his death, the fight over who would lead Islam between Sunni and Shia complicated matters and still does to this day. The word assassin itself comes from 11th century Shiites who were experts at killing Sunni.

In the 1450s, another advancement, the movable printing press, allowed the mass creation of books. Books allowed the rapid transfer and advancement of knowledge.

Beforehand, monks worked tirelessly on copying religious writings. This massive expansion of knowledge triggered the Renaissance. The Renaissance started as a cultural movement in Italy in the Late Medieval period and later spread to art, architecture, politics, science, and literature, marking the beginning of the Early Modern Age.

The modern principles of electricity generation, discovered during the early 1800s, allowed the harnessing of computers and communication.
In the current day, these tools are the key to sharing moments and knowledge. With this ability and the advancement of computers, we fueled a rapid expansion of knowledge.

Computers created a binary language which allowed miniaturization and automation through electrical currents.

Unfortunately, with this expansion, we have had several threats to our existence with war, terrorism, and individual sovereignty.

Early divisions between the Eastern and Western world seemed to divide over religion and customs. The Greeks vs. Persians was a battle between Western and Eastern society, which stopped the forceful spread of Islam to the West. The Spanish and Christian inquisitions were designed to kill and intimidate non-Christian believers. Martin Luther split Christianity over the thought that you had to pay for the redemption of your sins. The crusades were an attempt to spread Christianity and maintain control of the Holy Land in the Middle East through Jerusalem.

Conflicts between governments and religions over time have proven long lasting. Islam vs. Christianity during the Middle Ages, socialism vs. communism/capitalism during the world wars, and capitalism vs. communism during the Cold War.

With cheap energy being the fuel for economic growth and the foundation of your military industrial complex, conflicts over oil and energy have become the status quo. With the Middle East having the largest oil reserves, proxy wars and nation-building are gripping the planet and our expanding energy needs.

Chapter 5: You should know

There are some key concepts that I find to be vital for understanding the world around us.

How do we become who we are? What will we like? What do we believe? This formation of beliefs is called socialization. This lifelong process of inheriting and disseminating customs, values, and ideologies provide an individual with the skills and habits they use to participate in society. Though primarily learned from your parents at a young age, the interaction among your peers is playing an ever increasing role in beliefs and development.

Why do we make the decisions we do? There lies a rudimentary answer that applies in most situations: Maslow's hierarchy needs, in which we act based on the fulfillment of such needs. This theory has been updated and criticized, but I believe some concepts and principles do in fact occupy our decision-making paradigm. We're grouped into subsets of what we strive to achieve in a hierarchal order. First "physiological," then "safety," then "love," then "esteem," and then "self-actualization."

Physiological needs are those of the most basic: Food, water, things that we need to survive. When you don't have these, you will do anything you can to acquire them, with morality taking the backseat. With the advent of modern corporations, these needs have become easier and easier to fulfill, at least here in the United States.

Next, comes your safety. Are you comfortable in your surroundings? Can you eat? Sleep? Live life without being at risk? For example, if you live in a bad neighborhood that has shootings monthly, are you going to feel comfortable letting your child go outside and play? You work your hardest to head to a safer environment after your physiological needs are satisfied.

After our physiological needs
are met and we reside in a safe
environment, we look for love and
belongingness. Now, this area I believe
has changed over time with the
evolving culture of sexuality and
transition to a goods and material-
based society.

Love and belongingness used
only to apply to feelings connected to
your peers with similar interests. In the
modern age, I believe this need has
become difficult to satisfy sexually with
companionship. In regards to love, sex
is now also tied to this satisfaction of
love. Sex is more often used for
pleasure, often only agreeing to
engage once the material goods are

on an equal or desired level. Love and sex have always been two parts to fulfilling one need. You will not be satisfied with sex without love or love without sex.

The need to match our neighbors and have what they own has become a way of feeling like we belong. Our material goods must match the things others associate us with. We have to have this gadget, that car, this house.

In my view, more and more Americans are getting stuck in this situation as they try to work toward the needs of meeting the right life partner or having more luxury goods.

Who posts more on social media? Who has the cooler events? Who goes to the wildest places? Who can get more people to follow him or her? Who can get the most likes and retweets? There is an ongoing virtual amateur popularity contest. These two combinations of a lifelong quest for the right partner and ongoing popularity contest has prevented most from acting for anything but.

Once you're not making decisions to satisfy these needs, you've moved into the self-absorbed role of self-esteem. Your actions are not only for personal gain, safety, survival or to love and belong, but they are done to self-reflect on how others perceive you. Your esteem is a delicate balance to achieve. Too much self-promotion and you tread into areas of narcissism; too little, and you are not confident enough to earn the esteem of your peers. More often than not, it's impossible to maintain love and belongingness while acting for esteem, and not fall below acting toward another need.

Very few, as I call them, scholars have made it to self-actualization. This is truly realizing one's full potential. When you are acting with all of the previous needs satisfied, this is when your decisions become the ideal ones, able to stand the brutal test of quality and the good of the many over the needs of the few. Most often, those who approach self-actualization often search for ways to satisfy esteem as the complex nature of fulfilling love changes over time. We've seen a sharp decline in those who are self-actualized as we've advanced austerity in knowledge, schools, and learning.

The few remaining scholars are relics, most often getting to this point through years of experience, wisdom, and education, with financial and relationship luck. Age itself is a timeless issue that plays into most important decisions and understandings in life. So, how old is something? How old are you? How do we know?

Thankfully, with the advancement of modern science, we can answer this question -- Radio Active Carbon dating. Developed in the 1940's and winning the Nobel Peace prize, this theory is based on fundamental facts we have learned about our environment.

The carbon cycle again is the biogeochemical cycle by which carbon is exchanged amongst the environment. Radiocarbon dating is based on the fact that the sun produces cosmic rays that interact with nitrogen in the atmosphere. This carbon then is absorbed by photosynthesis into plants. When the organic material dies, it stops absorbing carbon. Over time, carbon decays in the material and can be measured by its decrease over time. Current methods can measure up to 50,000 years old. We can look at soil and rock layers to determine the history of our planet beyond the age of something individually.

This information is no secret. How

is it not spread, and why don't most people know it? The answer lies in several layers, each with profound implications. Religion has often fought the spread of knowledge over time as traditions and customs questioned. Leaders have often sought to control nations by restricting knowledge or insisting on the belief of one. The Internet has exploded the availability of knowledge but also works to legitimize opinions not founded in fact. Social media has allowed us not to have to question our beliefs by organizing in groups that make us complacent to the status quo.

Chapter 6: an American Century

From the time our country was founded, we have had great leaders accomplish amazing things to advance our society. These role models and legends fueled our ambitions while government provided a structure of opportunity. The very fabric of this society is being attacked by the lack of effective legislative policy. We don't need a revolution or radicals. We need reform. Our system was thought up by generations of men who escaped and studied history over time to enact policy to support and protect the people. We must now do the same.

To truly accomplish this, we must take a hard look at campaign financing – the funding that politicians use to become our elected representatives. No longer are we putting the best and the brightest forward, but the most well connected and elite. Donors dictate politicians' standings and action on issues, rather than the merit of what's best for our country. The more we allow money to dictate this political process, the more slanted legislation becomes to the powerful. Citizens United was a step in the wrong direction. Bundlers are a step in the wrong direction. Allowing influence by financial status is a step in the wrong direction. We need to pay our politicians more and take the donors more and more out of the process. We must enact strict individual contribution limits. Take corporations out of the political process entirely.

Taxes are one of the vital components to a functioning society. Our tax dollars go to pay for our stability, safety and security. The stronger the foundation in which we grow, the more stable and long-lasting success we will have. Currently, the tax code is a mess. Corporations and the wealthy are avoiding hundreds of billion in taxes with offshore tax shelters with manipulated deductions. Corporations keep offshore profits overseas, avoid paying domestic tax rates and abuse subsidies with tax avoidance. The wealthy hide and move their income as frequently as possible in any way they can pay the least tax.

To fix our tax code, we need to eliminate the advantages money can buy to avoid tax responsibility. US Corporations that earn money overseas should pay a flat tax on that money. Any corporation that sells products to US consumers should have to pay federal income tax regardless of what state or country it is based in. We need to raise taxes on those who make over $250,000 and take a long look at every deduction and subsidy the wealthy and corporations redeem.

Meanwhile, our justice system is backlogged, unfair and politically slanted. The wealthy can drown their opponents with paperwork. Public defenders have little resources and time. Judges are overwhelmed with caseloads. Jails are filled to capacity and politicians are in the pockets of private jail owners. We need to federalize the jail system, hire more judges and public defenders, and focus on rehabilitation and restitution, not incarceration for victimless or non-violent crime.

Unfortunately, financial inequality in and of itself spreads like disease into every facet of life. The workers' minimum wage has stayed stagnant while their productivity explodes.

Women's bodies are under assault by those who wish to control their actions and deny science. Minorities are blamed as the cause of economic and social problems. Seniors and immigrants are marginalized by their usefulness. Raise the minimum wage, strengthen affirmative action laws for all minorities, increase social service funding for the poor and elderly, bring the 14 million Americans already living here out of the shadows into our tax and legal system.

Many decry the government as a barrier to growth when in fact it can be a very powerful tool for good. We just need to change the way we spend money. Return on investment can no longer just be looked at by the impact on the dollar return itself but rather by the public good and saving that ensues. We need to move government work back to 100% contract bidding, no more pay-to-play favors. We need to de-burden small business from crushing regulation while enact more controls on larger corporations.

When you have a healthy, happy, and productive society, you have a growing economy. When you have a growing economy, you have a strong nation. Invest in our dilapidated infrastructure once and for all, fix our roads and bridges, modernize transportation services to include high-speed rail, and invest heavily in green, renewable energy initiatives. Teach our children to again reach for the stars by revolutionizing our space program and sending a manned mission to Mars. Offer free in-state tuition to college. Raise a tolerant, educated foundation for our future.

Well, I hope you've enjoyed this quick, guided tour. Stay tuned for the next part of this journey I wish to take you on in my sequel book, **Issue by Issue – A Hard Look at Your Political Beliefs.**

References

1: UN World Meteorological Organisation

2: WWF and the Zoological Society of London

3: Ecologist Mark Urban findings published in Science

4: Dr. James Hansen Goddard Institute for Space Studies

5: U.S. National Oceanic and Atmospheric Administration (NOAA)

6: United Nations and Who Owns the Water – Lars Muller Publishers

7: National Geographic: The Hidden Water We Use

8: Human Development Report 2006.

UNDP, 2006 and Coping with water scarcity. Challenge of the twenty-first century. UN-Water, FAO, 2007

9: NRDC: Water Pollution

10: Jay Famiglietti. Senior water scientist at NASA Jet Propulsion Laboratory/Caltech and Professor Earth system science at UC Irvine

11: AMA: American Medical Association

12: Inequality.org

13: Michael Moore verified by Politifact

14: Oxfam

15: FEC Data

16: Open Secrets

17: U.S. Office of Management and

Budget and Center on Budget and Policy Priorities

18: Citizens for Tax Justice

19: Tax Foundation

20: US National Debt Clock

21: National Center for Education Statistics and The National Center for Children in Poverty (NCCP)

22: Fortune 500 analysis by CNN and Huffington Post

23: Small Business Administration

24: Social Security Administration

25: Inside Edition

26: Wikipedia Christian Inquisition Aggregates

27: History Channel

28: Muslims Are Not Terrorists: A Factual Look at Terrorism and Islam